A Little Jazz Mass

Bob Chilcott

for mixed voices, piano, and optional bass and drum kit

Vocal score

MUSIC DEPARTMENT

OXFORD
UNIVERSITY PRESS

OXFORD
UNIVERSITY PRESS

Great Clarendon Street, Oxford OX2 6DP, England
198 Madison Avenue, New York, NY 10016, USA

Oxford University Press is a department of the University of Oxford.
It furthers the University's aim of excellence in research, scholarship,
and education by publishing worldwide in

Oxford New York
Auckland Cape Town Hong Kong Karachi
Kuala Lumpur Madrid Melbourne Mexico City Nairobi
New Delhi Shanghai Taipei Toronto

With offices in

Argentina Austria Brazil Chile Czech Republic France Greece
Guatemala Hungary Italy Japan Poland Portugal Singapore
South Korea Switzerland Thailand Turkey Ukraine Vietnam

Oxford is a registered trade mark of Oxford University Press
in the UK and in certain other countries

ISBN 978-0-19-335617-7

Music origination by
Enigma Music Production Services, Amersham, Bucks.
Printed in Great Britain on acid-free paper by
Halstan & Co. Ltd., Amersham, Bucks.

Contents

Composer's note

A Little Jazz Mass was originally written for upper voices and was first performed at the 2004 Crescent City Choral Festival, New Orleans, in June of that year.

I have always loved jazz. At the beginning of my writing career I worked from time to time as an arranger for the now defunct BBC Radio Orchestra and, while a member of the King's Singers, I was lucky enough to perform with such artists as George Shearing, Richard Rodney Bennett, John Dankworth, Art Farmer, and the WDR Big Band. These experiences and influences have all had an impact on the music that I compose.

In this mass setting I have written a piano part which may be played exactly as written. However, I would encourage the pianist to improvise freely on the chord structure, and would also encourage the addition of bass and drums and any other instruments that may be appropriate for the performance.

I am grateful to Cheryl Dupont, the conductor of the New Orleans Children's Chorus, for enabling this work to come to life in such a great jazz city, and to all the children in the Crescent City Choral Festival Choir 2004, who gave it such a great start. I am also grateful to Neil Richardson, a wonderful musician who, more than twenty years ago, gave me my first opportunity as a professional arranger at the BBC.

A notated bass part, with chord symbols, is available to purchase from the publisher (ISBN 978-0-19-335655-9).

The original version of this piece for upper voices (SSA) is also available to purchase (ISBN 978-0-19-343328-1).

Duration: c.12 minutes

A Little Jazz Mass

BOB CHILCOTT

1. *Kyrie*

*The piano part can be played as written or used as a guide. Bass and drum kit can join ad lib.

OXFORD UNIVERSITY PRESS, MUSIC DEPARTMENT, GREAT CLARENDON STREET, OXFORD OX2 6DP

-e e - le - i - son,_____ Chri - ste, Chri - ste, Chri - ste e-

-le - i - son, Chri - ste, Chri - ste, Chri - ste e - le - i - son,_____

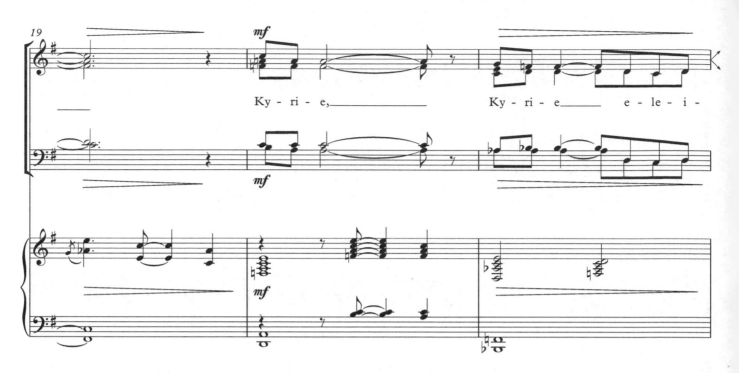

poco rit.

poco rit.

attacca

2. *Gloria*

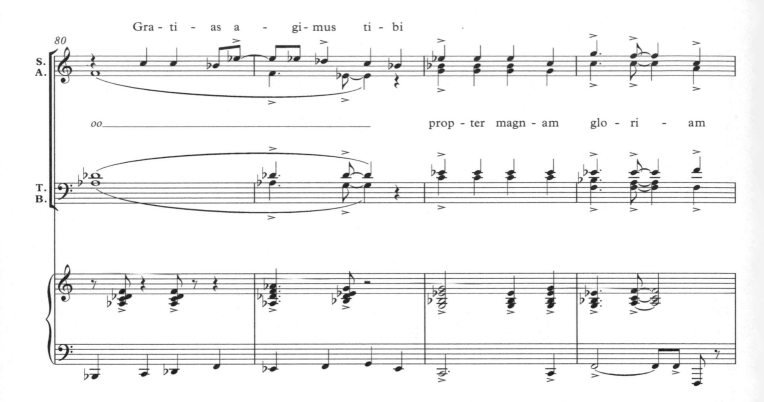

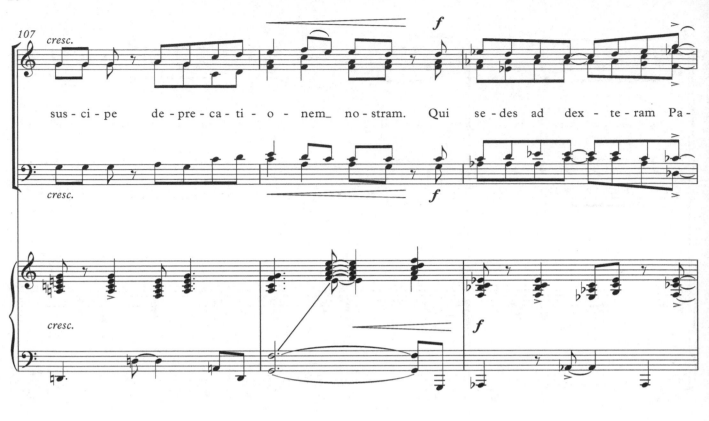

sus-ci-pe   de-pre-ca-ti-o-nem_ no-stram.   Qui se-des ad dex-te-ram Pa-

-tris,_____   mi-se-re-re,   mi - se - re - re_ no-bis._____

(pick up in new tempo)

22

Quo - ni - am Tu___ so - lus san - ctus, quo - ni - am.

Tu so - lus, so - lus Do - mi - nus,

oo_____

Tu so - lus al - tis - si - mus,

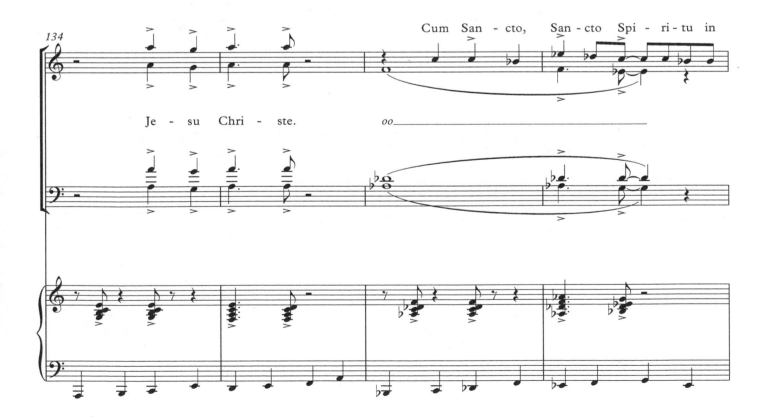

glo - ri - a De - i Pa - tris. A - men, a - men.

3. *Sanctus*

San - ctus, San - ctus Do - mi - nus, San - ctus,

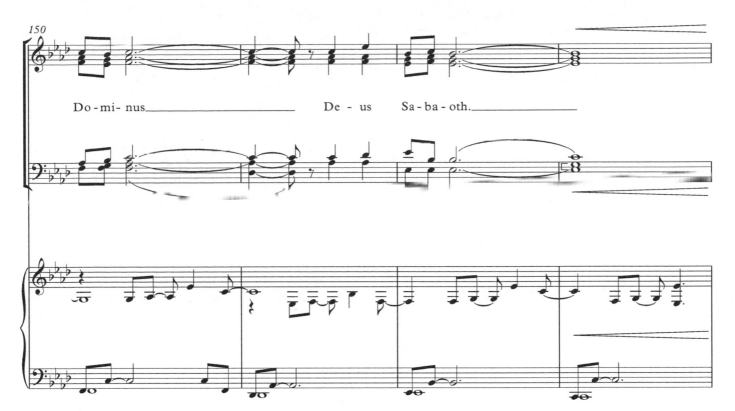

Do - mi - nus_____ De - us Sa - ba - oth._____

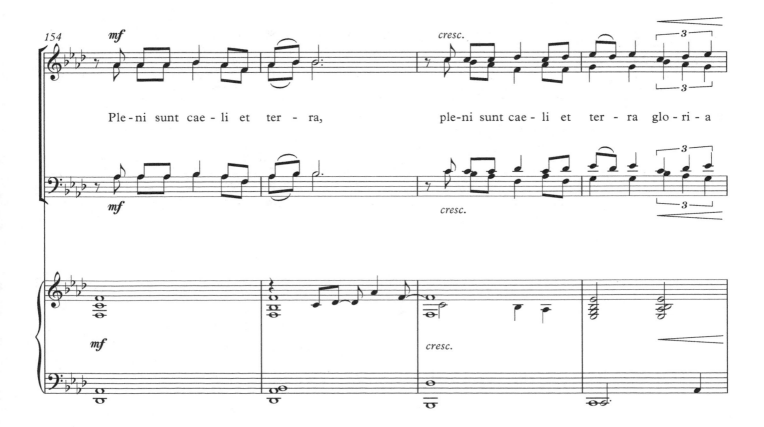

Ple - ni sunt cae - li et ter - ra, ple-ni sunt cae - li et ter - ra glo - ri - a

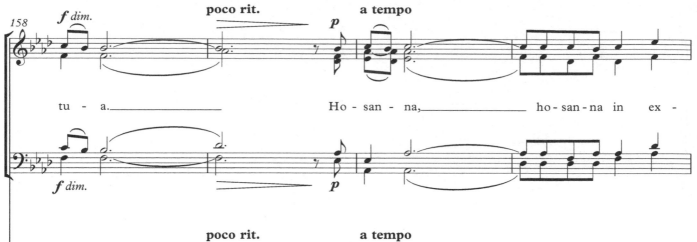

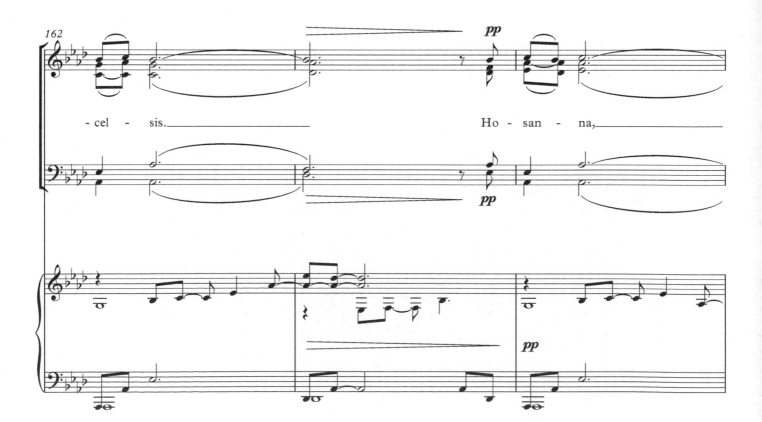

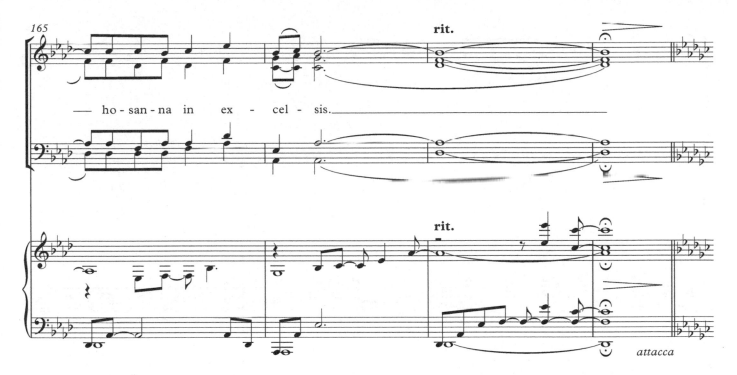

ho - san - na in ex - cel - sis.

4. *Benedictus*

Easy tempo ♩ = *c.*108

Be - ne - dic - tus,__ be - ne - dic -tus qui ve - nit__ in

-san - na in ex - cel - sis, in ex - cel - sis.

for Richard and Catherine Webber

5. *Agnus Dei*

Bluesy feel ♩ = *c.*63

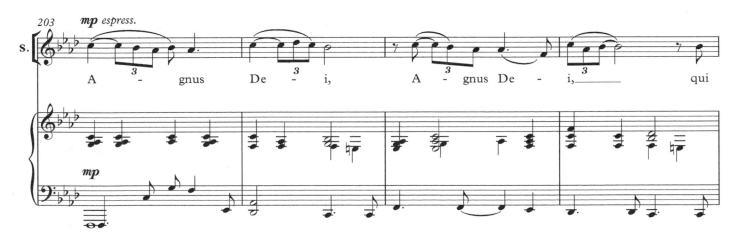

A - gnus De - i, A - gnus De - i,_____ qui

*If playing this movement with bass, the first four bars should be played as a piano solo, with the bass entering at bar 203.

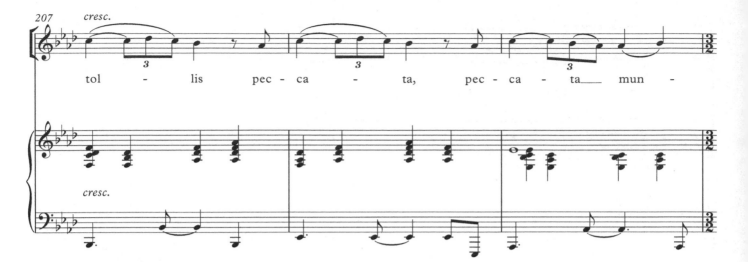

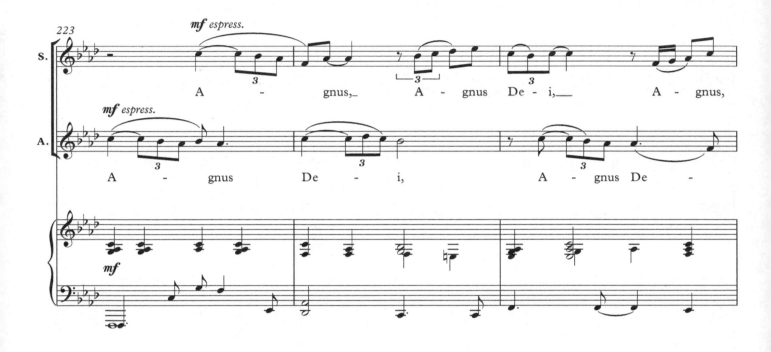

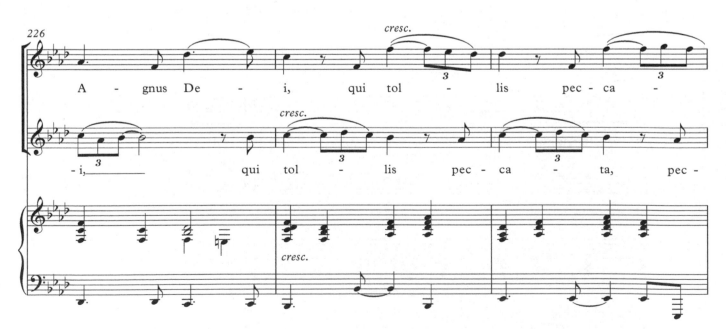

*If playing with bass, omit the piano left hand in bars 219–222 to allow a bass solo. The left hand re-enters at bar 223.

A - gnus De - i, qui tol-lis pec - ca - ta mun-di, mun - di,

tol - lis, qui tol - lis pec - ca - ta mun-di,

tol - lis, qui tol-lis pec-ca-ta mun-di, pec - ca - ta mun-di,

tol - lis, qui tol - lis pec - ca - ta mun-di,

Do-na no-bis pa - cem, do-na no-bis pa - cem, pa -

Do-na no-bis pa-cem, do - na no-bis pa - cem, pa -

Do - na no - bis, do - na no - bis pa - cem, pa -

Do - na no - bis, do - na no - bis pa - cem, pa -

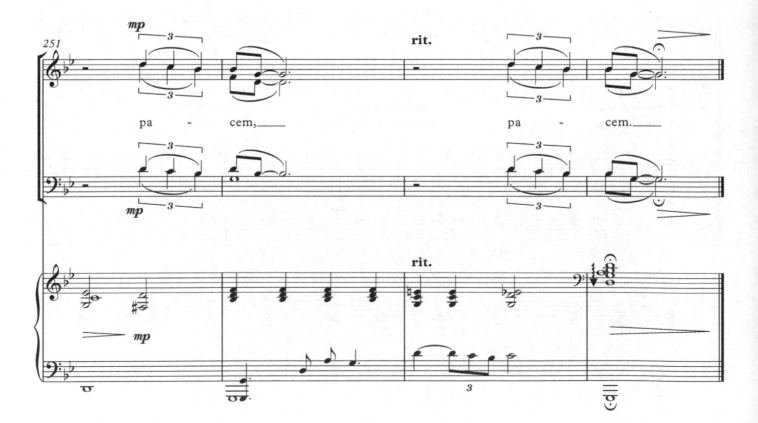

A Little Jazz Mass
instrumental accompaniment

Backing CD

This fantastic backing CD, recorded by a professional jazz trio, is ideal for use in both rehearsals and concerts. Compatible with the mixed-voice and upper-voice versions of *A Little Jazz Mass*, it is sure to inspire breathtaking performances from all choirs!

978-0-19-336382-3

Bass part

This bass part forms part of the jazz trio accompaniment and may be played as written or used as a guide from which the player may improvise freely. It is notated with chord symbols above the stave.

978-0-19-335655-9

The drummer should play along *ad lib.* –
a separate drumkit part is not provided